ALSO BY PAT ROSS

With Thanks & Appreciation
Formal Country
The Pleasure of Your Company
With Love & Affection
Motherly Devotion
I Thee Wed
To Have & to Hold

A Christmas Gathering

To _____

From _____

There seems a magic in the very name of Christmas.

—Charles Dickens
Sketches By Boz
1839

A Christmas Gathering

The Sweet Nellie Book of
Entertainment, Diversions, and Traditions
of the Holiday Season

PAT ROSS

VIKING
STUDIO
BOOKS

VIKING
Published by the Penguin Group
Viking Penguin, a division of Penguin Books USA Inc.,
375 Hudson Street, New York, New York 10014, U.S.A.
Penguin Books Ltd, 27 Wrights Lane, London W8 5TZ, England
Penguin Books Australia Ltd, Ringwood, Victoria, Australia
Penguin Books Canada Ltd, 10 Alcorn Avenue, Suite 300, Toronto, Ontario, Canada M4V 3B2
Penguin Books (N.Z.) Ltd, 182–190 Wairau Road, Auckland 10, New Zealand

Penguin Books Ltd, Registered Offices: Harmondsworth, Middlesex, England

First published in 1991 by Viking Penguin, a division of Penguin Books USA Inc.

1   3   5   7   9   10   8   6   4   2

Grateful acknowledgment is made for permission to reprint excerpts from
The Southern Christmas Book, by Harnett T. Kane. Copyright © 1958 by
Harnett T. Kane. Reprinted by permission of Harold Matson Company, Inc.
Grateful acknowledgment is made to the Kuenstler Archive for permission
to reprint the artwork on pages 20, 32, and 33.

LIBRARY OF CONGRESS CATALOGING IN PUBLICATION DATA
Ross, Pat, 1943–
A Christmas gathering: the Sweet Nellie book of entertainment,
diversions, and traditions of the holiday season/ Pat Ross.
p.   cm.
ISBN 0-670-83530-7
1. Christmas.   I. Title.
GT4985.R68   1991
394.2'68282 — dc20   91–50164

Printed in Singapore   Set in Nicholas Cochin   Designed by Amy Hill

AN APPRECIATION

Gifts are not always wrapped with colorful papers and tied with pretty bows. The most special offerings come in the no-frills form of tireless assistance, continuing good wishes, and cheerful moral support—the gifts that made this book possible.

My year-round appreciation to Leisa Crane for her keen and impressive research, to Susan Quick for handling the details so efficiently, and to the Sweet Nellie staff for making the shop's extended Christmas season merry and carefree. Mary Santangelo, Bonnie Ferriss, and Berta Montgomery continue to comb their antique paper collections, never running out of treasures.

The various librarians, ephemera collectors, and antiques dealers who continue to provide needed assistance have, by this sixth book, grown into a substantial list, making it difficult to mention each person by name. Much like Santa's elves, they are behind-the-scenes essentials.

There are always the "regulars": my supportive family; my agent, Amy Berkower; my editor, Barbara Williams, and publisher, Michael Fragnito, who, with their superb staff, continue to make the best books in town!

INTRODUCTION

Our Christmas traditions are richer than plum pudding. Whether the day itself is a lavish event or a simple gathering of family and friends, there are old memories to share and new ones to make. Wish-making—too often considered frivolous during the rest of the year—is suddenly acceptable for all ages. Grown-ups may still wish with a measure of reason, just in case, but a centuries-old St. Nicholas tradition has offered promise to children who make their wishing blatant and hopeful.

Over the years, poets and writers have penned tomes on the subject of Christmas. We are told how to plan a party, wrap a gift, and make the perfect punch. Celebration of the joy and spirit of the holiday are passed down to us through verses, letters, and novels. There is really no end to the material available; there is, unfortunately, a limit to the amount one can include in this small volume.

Poring through this recorded heritage, I was brought back to my own indelible Christmas memories. When I was a child, I always made an excessive wish list, hinting broadly about Christmas just as soon as the Thanksgiving dinner was cleared away. My younger sister used every trick in the book to steal peeks at my list and I hers, but we kept our hopes closely guarded.

When I was eight, I was certain life could not go on without the gorgeous "Pretty Polly" doll on display at the town's only hardware store, which doubled as the local gift bazaar during the holidays. Polly was a life-size blond fantasy with perfect features and a gown fit for royalty. My parents noticed her price tag, not her great beauty, and suggested a substitute for my list. The theatrics that followed are legendary in our family. They were wasted on my parents. But they touched my softhearted grandfather, who secretly bought two Pollys—one for me and her identical twin for Jeanne—and put them under our tree.

My wish came true, but it had its downside. This plastic beauty decked out in lace that scratched was too large to hold and too stiff to cuddle. She sat on my bed, decorative and unloved, until I retired her to the closet without a word. The warm memory I am left with today is not of the gift, but of the giver—a thoughtful and doting man who could not bear to see a child's heart broken. "Pretty Polly" became my most memorable gift.

A Christmas Gathering takes us back to memories, and to a time when a ringing phone did not disturb the tranquillity of the falling snow or the faraway sound of carolers coming to your house. It was a spirited time without distractions when the warmth of the season could be enjoyed for its own sake. So, before the mulled cider cools off, partake of this cheerful season and remember.

Twas the night before Christmas,
when all through the house
Not a creature was stirring,
not even a mouse.

—Clement Clarke Moore
"A Visit from St. Nicholas"
1823

*Christmas
Is Coming*

Coming! Ay, so is Christmas.

—Jonathan Swift
Polite Conversation
1738

Heap on more wood!—the wind is chill;
But let it whistle as it will,
We'll keep our Christmas merry still.

—Sir Walter Scott
"Marmion"
1808

Christmas is the anniversary of new winter bonnets in our goodly city.

—Godey's Lady's Book
1851

Please drop a note to the clerk of the weather, and have a good, rousing snowstorm—say, on the twenty-second. None of your meek, gentle, nonsensical, shilly-shallying snow-storms; not the sort where the flakes float lazily down from the sky as if they didn't care whether they ever got here or not, and then melt away as soon as they touch the earth, but a regular businesslike whizzing, whirring, blurring, cutting snow-storm, warranted to freeze and stay on!

—Kate Douglas Wiggin
The Birds' Christmas Carol
1886

"I have often thought," says Sir Roger, "it happens very well that Christmas should fall out in the middle of winter."

—Joseph Addison
The Spectator
January 8, 1712

At Christmas play and make good cheer,
For Christmas comes but once a year.

—Thomas Tusser
The Farmer's Daily Diet
1580

As well might we dance without music, or attempt to write a poem without rhythm, as to keep Christmas without a Christmas tree.

—*Weekly Press*
1877

O, Christmas Tree!

The tree was planted in the middle of a great round table, and towered high above their heads. It was brilliantly lighted by a multitude of little tapers; and everywhere sparkled and glittered with bright objects.

—Charles Dickens
A Christmas Tree
1850

She lit another match. This time she was sitting under a lovely Christmas tree. It was much bigger and more beautifully decorated than the one she had seen when she had peeped through the glass doors at the rich merchant's house this Christmas day. Thousands of lighted candles gleamed upon its branches, and coloured pictures such as she had seen in the shop windows looked down upon her.

—Hans Christian Andersen
The Little Match Girl
1846

'Ay, ay' . . . us old fellows wish ourselves young tonight, when we see the mistletoe bough in the White Parlor.

—George Eliot
Silas Marner
1851

The misletoe hung in the castle hall,
The holly branch shone on the old oak wall.

—Thomas Haynes Bayly
The Misletoe Bough
1844

A bayberry candle burned to the socket
Brings luck to the house and gold to the pocket.

—Anonymous

The tree, which stands upon a table covered with white damask, is supported at the root by piles of sweets of a larger kind, and by toys and dolls of all descriptions, suited to a youthful fancy.

—*Illustrated London News*
1848

Jo was the first to wake in the grey dawn of Christmas morning. No stockings hung at the fireplace, and for a moment she felt as much disappointed as she did long ago, when her little sock fell down because it was so crammed with goodies.

—Louisa May Alcott
Little Women
1868

First comes the stocking of little Nell;
Oh, dear Santa, fill it well;
Give her a dollie that laughs and cries
One that will open and shut her eyes.

—Benjamin Handby
"Up on the Housetop"
1864

Ho! Ho! Ho!

At Christmas Laugh
and make good cheer,
To welcome Father
Christmas

See! here Father
Christmas comes
To bring you toys and
sugar-plums

ot believe in Santa Claus! You might as well not believe in fairies. . . . Nobody sees Santa Claus, but that is no sign that there is no Santa Claus. The most real things in the world are those which neither children nor men can see. Thank God! he lives and he lives forever.

—Francis Church
"Is There a Santa Claus?"
New York Sun, September 21, 1897

Up on the housetop the reindeer pause,
Out jumps good old Santa Claus;
Down through the chimney with lots of toys,
All for the little ones, Christmas joys.

—Benjamin Handby
"Up on the Housetop"
1864

Of all animals of the deer kind, the Rein-Deer is the
most extraordinary and the most useful.

—Oliver Goldsmith
Natural History
1774

CALENDAR PAGE
FOR DECEMBER

Gentle, at home, amid
my friends I'll be
Like the high leaves
Upon the holly tree.

—*Godey's Lady's Book*
1890

PRESENTS WE DON'T WANT

(1) Chocolates with hard centers

(2) Bright cushions (that match nothing in the house)

(3) Complicated apparatus for licking stamps

(4) Fountain pens that leak

(5) Penwipers, biscuit barrels, useless ornaments
    in shapes of pigs, cats, etc.

(6) Bookends that are too light

(7) Dressing bags that are too heavy

—Rose Henniker Heaton
The Perfect Christmas
1933

CHRISTMAS GREETINGS
with love to Helen from Laura

A beautiful card is better than a rubbishy present, and at all events it doesn't involve a letter of thanks. It is a bad, bad plan to use up last year's card from returning it to the original sender, crossing "From Charles to Lottie" and simply substituting "*To* Charles *from* Lottie."

—Rose Henniker Heaton
The Perfect Christmas
1933

OLD SOUTHERN SUPERSTITIONS

It is a good idea to have every caller bring in a token gift, which may be practically anything: the end of a branch, a few pecans from your yard, your garden shears. Some people have been known to meet guests outside and hand them a little item to bring in, "just to make sure we have luck in this place."

—Harnett T. Kane
The Southern Christmas Book
1958

O you merry, merry Souls,
Christmas is a' coming,
We shall have flowing bowls,
Dancing, piping, drumming.

—*Christmas Entertainments*
1740

Gathered Together

Wednesday, December 25th, 1844. Clear and mild. . . . This is my first Christmas as a married woman, and housekeeper; for one month I have been married, and am very happy; but today I want to be at home with my dear Mother, my little Brothers, my sweet little Sister, fond Aunts and devoted Uncles—how they all pet and love me!

—From the diary of Mahala Eggleston Roach

The cock sat up in the yew tree,
The hen came chuckling by,
I wish you a merry Christmas
And a good fat pig in the sty.

—W.S.W. Anson, ed.
The Christmas Book of
Carols and Songs

Hallo! A great deal of steam! The pudding was out of the copper. A smell like a washing-day! That was the cloth. A smell like an eating-house and a pastrycook's next door to each other, with a laundress's next door to that! That was the pudding! ... Oh, what a wonderful pudding!

—Charles Dickens
A Christmas Carol
1843

Carol is the dearest part of Christmas to Uncle Jack, and he'll have none of it without her. She is better than all the turkeys and puddings and apples and spare ribs and wreaths and garlands and mistletoe and stockings and chimneys and sleigh-bells in Christendom. She is the very sweetest Christmas Carol that was ever written, said, sung, or chanted, and I am coming as fast as ships and railway trains can carry me to tell her so.

—Kate Douglas Wiggin
The Birds' Christmas Carol
1886

The only real blind person at Christmastime is he who has not Christmas in his heart.

—Helen Keller
The Ladies Home Journal
1906

A great deal of the comfort and satisfaction of a good dinner depends on the carving. Awkward carving is enough to spoil the appetite of a refined and sensitive person.

—*The Perfect Gentleman*
1860

I look for the time when we shall wish one another a Merry Christmas every morning; when roast turkey and plum pudding shall be the staple of our daily dinner, and the holly shall never be taken down from the walls, and everyone will always be kissing everyone else under the mistletoe.

—Max Beerbohm
A Christmas Garland
1912

There never was such a goose. Bob said he didn't believe there ever was such a goose cooked. Its tenderness and flavour, size and cheapness, were the themes of universal admiration.

—Charles Dickens
A Christmas Carol
1843

Christmas is coming, the geese are getting fat,
Please to put a penny in the old man's hat;
If you haven't got a penny, a ha'penny will do,
If you haven't got a ha'penny, God bless you!

—Beggar's rhyme

My Christmas day was without dinner or presents, for the first time since I can remember. Yet it has been a very memorable day, and I feel as if I'd had a splendid feast seeing the poor babies wallow in turkey soup, and that every gift I put into their hands had come back to me in the dumb delight of their unchild-like faces trying to smile.

—Louisa May Alcott
Life and Letters
1875

MENU FOR BOXING DAY

Will you try to persuade your guests, for the sake of their complexions, digestions, and tempers, to try the effect of a Fruit and Salad Day, in order to undo the ill effects of overeating the day before.

—Rose Henniker Heaton
The Perfect Christmas
1933

Here's to the day of good will, cold weather, and warm hearts!

—Anonymous

Celebration

Ah Bill, I shan't forget yer,
and I'll oftentimes recall
That lively gaited sworray—
The Cowboy's Christmas Ball.

—Larry Crittendon
The Cowboy's Christmas Ball
1891

As soon would he tolerate the mint being bruised in his julep as to allow anything in his eggnog but well-beaten eggs, sugar, and whiskey or brandy, mixed with rum. And he drank it from a silver spoon, as a gentleman should.

—Richard Henry Hutchings
1840s

Now thrice welcome, Christmas,
 Which brings us good cheer,
Minc'd pies and plumb-porridge,
 Good ale and strong beer;
With pig, goose, and capon,
 The best that may be,
So well doth the weather
 And our stomachs agree.

—Christmas Song
1695

A Merry Christmas

Here we come a-wassailing
Among the leaves so green;
Here we come a-wandering,
So fair to be seen:

Love and joy come to you,
And to your wassail too,
And God bless you, and send you
A happy new year.

—"The Wassail Song"
Yorkshire, 1850

TO YE FUTURE

JAN. 1ST

Ring out the old, ring in the new,
Ring, happy bells, across the snow:
The year is going, let him go;
Ring out the false, ring in the true.

—Alfred, Lord Tennyson
"In Memoriam A.H.H."
1851

Ring In the New

I don't know what to do!" cried Scrooge, laughing and crying in the same breath, and making a perfect Laocoön of himself with his stockings. "I am as light as a feather. I am as happy as an angel, I am as merry as a schoolboy. I am as giddy as a drunken man. A merry Christmas to everybody! A happy New Year to all the world! Hallo here! Whoop! Hallo!"

—Charles Dickens
A Christmas Carol
1843

A happy New Year to You!

God bless the master of this house,
The mistress also,
And all the little children,
That round the table go,
And all your kin and kinsmen,
That dwell both far and near,
I wish you a merry Christmas
And a happy New Year.

—Anonymous Christmas carol

COMMON SUPERSTITIONS

Wear something fresh and new on Christmas Day—your luck will improve. But don't wear new shoes. At best they will hurt like fury, at worst they will walk you into a catastrophe.

If you leave a loaf of bread on the table after Christmas Eve supper, you will be sure to have a full supply until the next Christmas.

Eat apples as the clock strikes midnight on Christmas Eve. This will guarantee perfect health for the year ahead.

On New Year's Eve, a few minutes before midnight, throw open every door and window, no matter what the weather— rain, snow, sleet, or wind. The good results will justify any exposure short of fatal pneumonia.

—Harnett T. Kane
The Southern Christmas Book
1958

My song is done, I must be gone.
I can stay no longer here.
God bless you all, both great and small,
And send you a happy New Year!

—W.S.W. Anson, ed.
*The Christmas Book of
Carols and Songs*

It seems fitting that a book about traditions of the past should be decorated with period artwork. In that spirit, the art in *A Christmas Gathering* has been taken from personal collections of original nineteenth- and early twentieth-century Christmas cards, calling cards, party invitations, etchings, book illustrations, and other paper treasures of the time.

The endpapers and chapter openings contain a pattern reproduced from one of our favorite vintage wallpapers.